HIDING IN
OCEANS

Deborah Underwood

www.raintreepublishers.co.uk
Visit our website to find out more information about Raintree books.

To order:
☎ Phone 0845 6044371
🖷 Fax +44 (0) 1865 312263
🖳 Email myorders@raintreepublishers.co.uk

Customers from outside the UK please telephone +44 1865 312262

Raintree is an imprint of Capstone Global Library Limited, a company incorporated in England and Wales having its registered office at 7 Pilgrim Street, London, EC4V 6LB – Registered company number: 6695582

Text © Capstone Global Library Limited 2011
First published in hardback in 2011
The moral rights of the proprietor have been asserted.

Edited by Rebecca Rissman and Nancy Dickmann
Designed by Joanna Hinton Malivoire
Picture research by Tracy Cummins
Originated by Capstone Global Library
Printed and bound in China by Leo Paper Products Ltd

ISBN 978 0 431 01063 2
15 14 13 12 11
10 9 8 7 6 5 4 3 2 1

British Library Cataloguing in Publication Data
Underwood, Deborah.
  Hiding in oceans. -- (Creature camouflage)
  1. Marine animals--Juvenile literature. 2. Camouflage (Biology)--Juvenile literature.
  I. Title II. Series
  591.4'72'09162-dc22

Acknowledgements
We would like to thank the following for permission to reproduce photographs: Getty Images pp. 7 (Jeff Foott), 8 (Karan Kapoor), 10 (Mark Deeble and Victoria Stone), 11, 12 (David B. Fleetham), 29 (Peter David); National Geographic Stock pp. 17, 18 (Mauricio Handler); nautrepl.com pp. 9 (© David Fleetham), 13, 14, 23, 24 (© Jurgen Freund), 19, 20 (© Brent Hedges), 27 (© Doug Perrine); Photolibrary pp. 6, 21, 22, 25, 26 (David B Fleetham); Shutterstock pp. 4 (© Map Resources), 5, 15, 26 (© Rich Carey), 28 (© melissaf84).

Cover photograph of a pair of cuttlefish (Sepia pharaonis III) on tropical coral reef, used with permission of Getty Images (Jeff Hunter).

We would like to thank Michael Bright for his invaluable help in the preparation of this book.

Every effort has been made to contact copyright holders of any material reproduced in this book. Any omissions will be rectified in subsequent printings if notice is given to the publisher.

All the Internet addresses (URLs) given in this book were valid at the time of going to press. However, due to the dynamic nature of the Internet, some addresses may have changed, or sites may have changed or ceased to exist since publication. While the author and publisher regret any inconvenience this may cause readers, no responsibility for any such changes can be accepted by either the author or the publisher.

Contents

Some words are printed in bold, **like this**. You can find out what they mean by looking in the glossary.

What are oceans like?

Oceans are huge areas of salty water. Oceans cover most of the Earth. There are five main oceans on Earth.

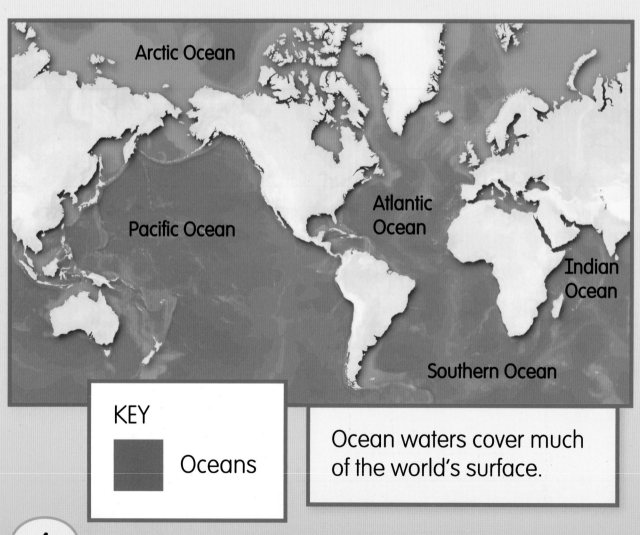

Arctic Ocean

Pacific Ocean

Atlantic Ocean

Indian Ocean

Southern Ocean

KEY

Oceans

Ocean waters cover much of the world's surface.

Oceans are home to many different kinds of animals.

Oceans are important to life on Earth. Plant-like living things in the ocean help make the air we breathe. The ocean affects Earth's weather. Many animals depend on food from the ocean.

Living in the ocean

Oceans are full of life. Ocean animals can be tiny or huge. Some ocean animals move around to find food. Some wait for food to come to them.

The blue whale is the world's largest animal.

Manatees have flat tails that help them move through the water.

All ocean animals have special **features** to help them **survive** in water. These features are called **adaptations**.

What is camouflage?

Camouflage is an **adaptation** that helps animals hide. An animal's colour or shape can help it hide. The way an animal behaves can help it hide, too. Why do you think animals need to hide?

Some animals have clear bodies that make them hard to see in the water.

Can you see the scorpionfish hiding in this picture?

Animals that eat other animals are called **predators**. Being able to hide makes them better hunters.

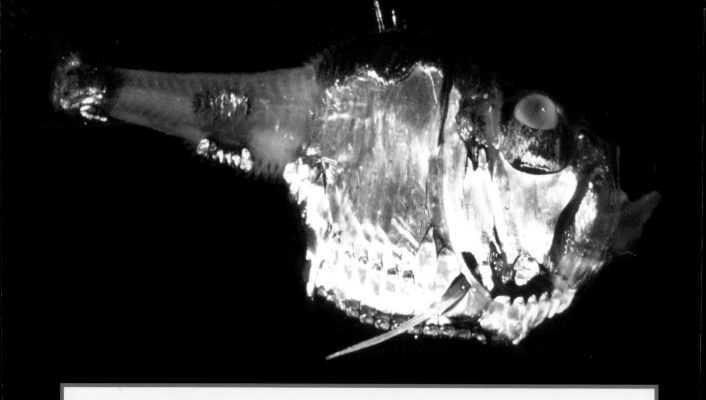

Hatchetfish can make their bellies glow! This helps hide them from fish swimming below. The fish think they are looking at sunlight.

Animals that **predators** eat are called **prey**. Prey animals hide so they won't become a predator's lunch!

Find the ocean animals

Longnose hawkfish

Longnose hawkfish have red lines on their bodies. They have long snouts, and **spines** on their top **fins**.

CAMOUFLAGED

Longnose hawkfish often hide in animals called sea fans. Some sea fans have thin, red branches. The red lines on the fish's body help it to look like the sea fan.

REVEALED

Decorator crab

The decorator crab is a **camouflage** expert! The crab finds small animals and bits of seaweed. It sticks them all over its shell. This helps the crab to hide.

When a decorator crab gets too big for its shell, the old shell comes off. A new, bigger shell grows. Then the crab moves the animals and seaweed from the old shell to the new one!

REVEALED

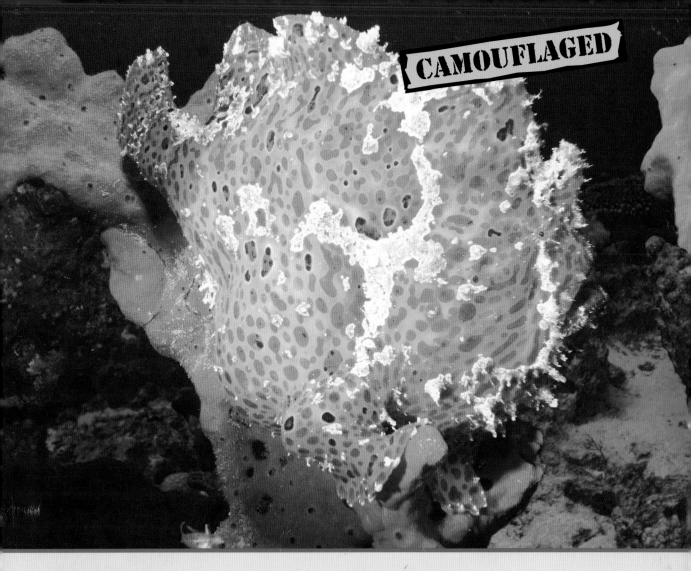

Frogfish

There are many types and colours of frogfish. They can look like sponges, corals, or seaweeds. This helps them hide while they wait for **prey**.

A frogfish has a **spine** that sticks out from its head. It can wiggle the spine. The spine looks like food to other fish. When **prey** comes close, the frogfish chomps!

spine

REVEALED

CAMOUFLAGED

Great white shark

The back of a great white shark is a dark colour. A prey animal swimming above the shark would not easily spot it. The shark's dark back **blends in** with the bottom of the ocean.

The great white shark has a light belly. **Prey** swimming below the shark might not see it. The shark's light belly looks like sunlight on the sea.

REVEALED

Leafy sea dragon

Leafy sea dragons use their colour and shape for **camouflage**. Leaf-like parts stick out from their bodies. The sea dragons look like seaweed!

Leafy sea dragons do not have teeth. They wait until **prey** comes close to them. Then they suck up the prey with their tube-shaped snouts.

REVEALED

Peacock flounder

Peacock flounders live on the ocean floor. They change their colours to match the things around them. They even change the **patterns** on their skin!

Peacock flounders also bury themselves in the sand. Only their eyes stick up. Each eye can look in a different direction at the same time! The flounders watch for **prey** that swims by.

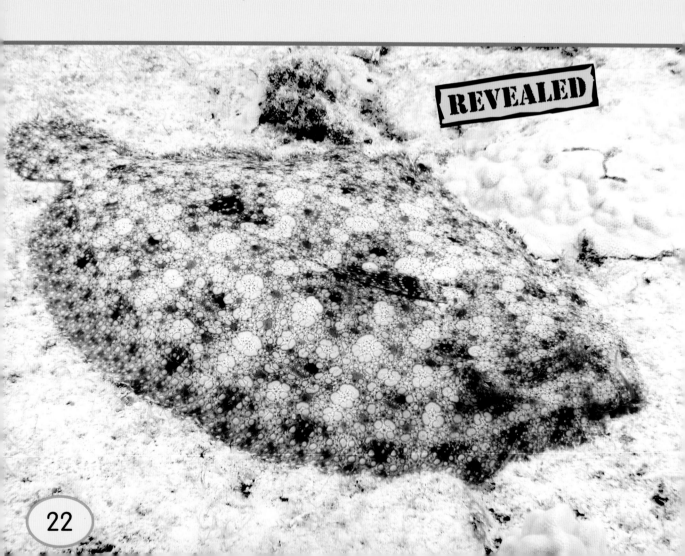

REVEALED

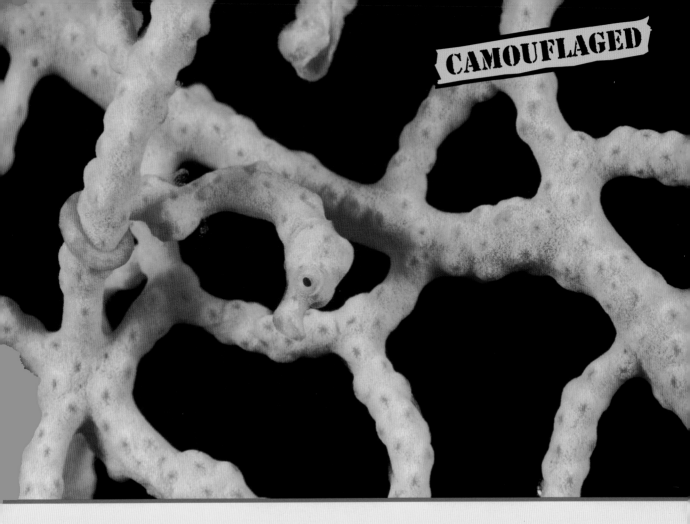

Pygmy seahorse

Pygmy seahorses are only about 2½ centimetres long! They live among underwater animals called coral. The seahorses' colours and bumpy bodies match the coral they live on.

A pygmy seahorse's colour and bumps help to hide it from **predators**. Its **camouflage** helps it hide as it waits for food to pass by.

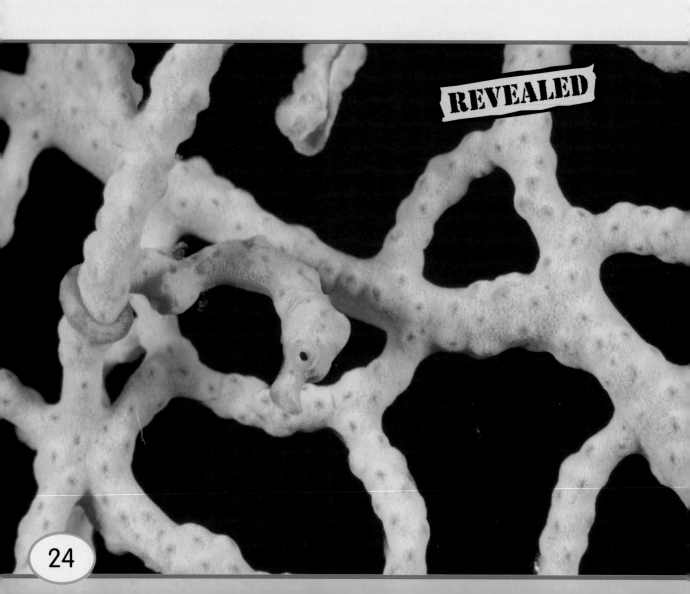

REVEALED

Two-spotted octopus

A two-spotted octopus has excellent camouflage! It can change its colour very quickly. The octopus **blends in** to hide from animals that might eat it.

A two-spotted octopus has another way to hide, too. If a **predator** comes close, the octopus squirts black ink into the water! The cloud of ink hides the octopus while it swims away.

REVEALED

These ghost pipefish look like pieces of sea grass floating in the water!

pipefish

sea grass

Some ocean animals **blend in** with the sea floor. Others hide in seaweed, rocks, or coral. **Camouflage** helps them to **survive** in their underwater homes.

Animals that stand out

The bright orange clownfish does not need **camouflage**. It lives inside a sea animal that has a **venomous** sting! But the clownfish has special skin. The venom cannot hurt the clownfish.

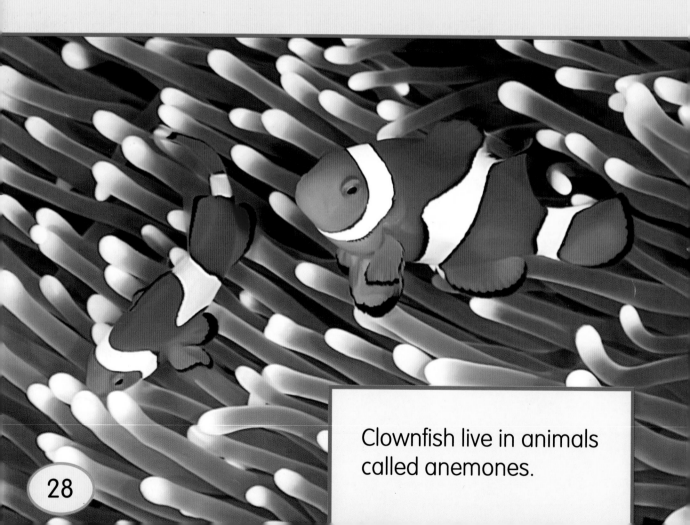

Clownfish live in animals called anemones.

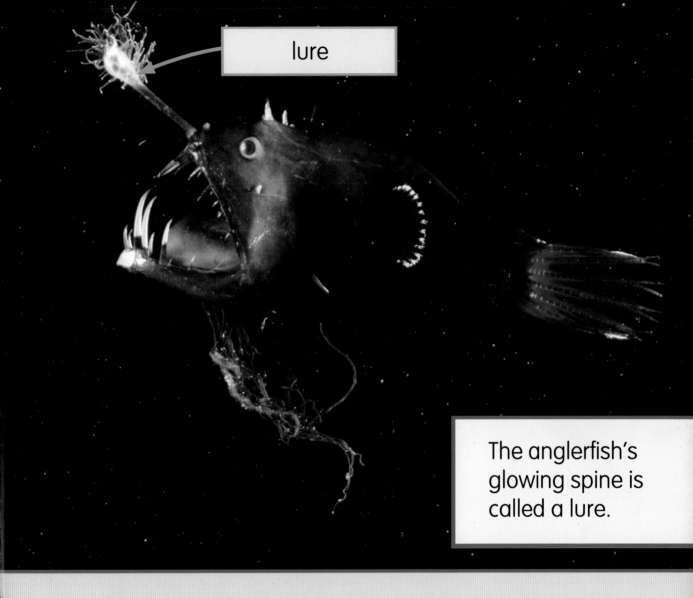

lure

The anglerfish's glowing spine is called a lure.

Anglerfish live deep in the ocean. An anglerfish has a glowing **spine** on its head. Other animals swim toward the light. Then the anglerfish eats them!

Glossary

adaptation special feature that helps an animal stay alive in its surroundings

blend in matches well with the things around it

camouflage adaptation that helps an animal blend in with its surroundings

feature special part of an animal

fin part of a fish that looks like a wing

pattern shapes and marks on an animal's body

predator animal that eats other animals

prey animal that other animals eat

spine pointed part of an animal, like a needle

survive stay alive

venomous something dangerous that can make you very ill, or even kill you

Find out more

Books to read

Extreme Habitats: Oceans, Susie Hodge
  (TickTock Media Ltd., 2007)

*Undersea Encounters: Survival Secrets of Sea
  Animals,* Mary Jo Rhodes (Scholastic, 2007)

Websites

**gowild.wwf.org.uk/gowild/happening_habitats/
oceans**
Visit the World Wildlife Fund's website for more
information about oceans.

www.nhm.ac.uk/kids-only/life/life-sea
Learn more fascinating facts about oceans and
ocean animals on the Natural History Museum's
Kids Only website.

Index